P9-CDZ-922

RON MILLER

VENUS

WORLDS BEYOND

TWENTY-FIRST CENTURY BOOKS   BROOKFIELD, CONNECTICUT

Dedicated to Kate Miller

Illustrations by Ron Miller. Photographs courtesy of NASA.

Library of Congress Cataloging-in-Publication Data
Miller, Ron, 1947–
Venus / by Ron Miller.
p. cm. – (Worlds beyond)
Include index.
Summary: Chronicles the discovery and explorations of the planet Venus and
discusses its composition, its place in the solar system, and more.
ISBN: 0-7613-2359-7 (lib. bdg.)
1. Venus (Planet)—Juvenile literature. [1. Venus (Planet)] I. Title.
QB621 .M55 2002   523.42 — 2   2001036791

Published by Twenty-First Century Books
A Division of The Millbrook Press, Inc.
2 Old New Milford Road
Brookfield, CT 06804
www.millbrookpress.com

CONTENTS

The astronomical symbol for Venus

A symbolic image of
Venus as the goddess of
love and beauty

CHAPTER ONE

THE MYSTERIOUS PLANET

Venus was the Morning and Evening Star of ancient civilizations such as those of the Greeks, Romans, and Babylonians. It outshines every other body in the sky, except for the Sun and the Moon. Sometimes it is even bright enough to cast faint shadows. Its brilliant gleaming in the twilight or dawn skies inspired the Romans to name it Venus, for their goddess of love and beauty. Even earlier than that it was known to the Babylonians as Ishtar —for their Earth mother, goddess of love and marriage. The Phoenicians called the planet Astarte, for their goddess of love and fertility, and to the Greeks she was Aphrodite, for their goddess of beauty and love. Because it was considered such a bright, beautiful star, ancient astrologers thought that Venus embodied gentleness and charm, love and beauty, music and dance.

When the planet Venus appeared in the dawn sky before sunrise, the Greeks called it Phosphorus, the Bringer of Light. When Venus followed the Sun as it sank beneath the horizon, they called it Hesperus, from their word for *western* or *evening*. These were thought to be two different stars until the Greek geometer Pythagoras concluded, around 500 B.C., that they are one and the same.

Some say Venus, the goddess of love and beauty, was the daughter of Jupiter and Dione. Others say that Venus sprang from the foam of the sea. The wind wafted her along the waves to the Isle of Cyprus, where she was received and attired by the Seasons, and then led to the assembly of the gods. All were charmed with her beauty, and each one demanded her for his wife. Jupiter gave her to Vulcan, the homeliest of the gods, in gratitude for the service he had rendered in forging thunderbolts. So the most beautiful of the goddesses became the wife of the most ill-favored of gods.

Venus possessed an embroidered belt called Cestus, which had the power of inspiring love. Her favorite birds were swans and doves, and the plants sacred to her were the rose and the myrtle. Eros, the god of love, was the son of Venus. He was her constant companion, and, armed with bow and arrows, he shot the darts of desire into the bosoms of both gods and men.

—Adapted from *Bulfinch's Mythology* (1855)

The Venus of classical mythology, as depicted in a nineteenth-century engraving

Venus is Earth's sister planet. It is almost exactly the same size as our planet, and its orbit is closer to our planet than that of any other planet in our solar system. Of all the worlds in the solar system, it should most resemble our own planet. But neither Venus's beauty nor its apparent similarity to Earth prepared anyone for what the planet is really like. It was as though Venus wore a beautiful mask, hiding a face that was anything but beautiful.

The slow realization of the true nature of Venus began in the year 1610, when the Italian astronomer Galileo Galilei first turned a telescope toward the night sky. The telescope had been invented in the Netherlands a few years earlier, but it was used almost exclusively for terrestrial observation. No one had thought of using the telescope at night to look at the Moon or stars. And why should they? To the best of anyone's knowledge, the stars were nothing more than brilliant points of light—they weren't considered tangible objects. Nor did anyone think there was anything particularly unusual about the five bright stars called planets, other than that, unlike other stars, they moved slowly among their fixed neighbors. The word *planet* originally meant *wanderer*, referring to their slow movement through the sky. It was only after Galileo's discoveries that *planet* came to have the modern meaning of *world*.

When Galileo looked at Venus with his telescope, he was surprised not to see a star at all. Through a telescope a star looks like a brilliant point of light, but what Galileo saw looked instead like a gleaming pearl: a round, white sphere that was clearly another world in space. Most important, from Galileo's point of view, was that Venus showed **phases**, like Earth's Moon. This proved that

In ancient Greece, Venus was known as the
Morning or Evening star, depending on where
it was in its orbit. It appears as a very bright
star, often outshining every other object in the
sky except for the Sun and the Moon.

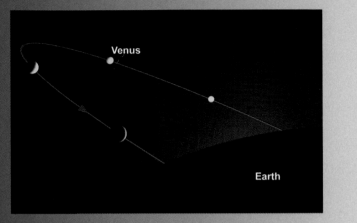

PHASES

As Venus circles the Sun, we see it lit from different angles. This causes Venus to show phases like our Moon. For example, when Venus is between the Sun and Earth, we see it only as a thin crescent because the unlit back side of the planet is facing us. When Venus is on the other side of the Sun from Earth, we can see its fully lit side. In between we see different crescent phases of Venus. Oddly enough, Venus is brighter in our sky when it is in its crescent phase than when it is full. Because Venus is so much closer when it is a crescent, the illuminated part we see is much larger than the more distant full phase.

Venus orbited around the Sun and not Earth, supporting the radical new theory of Nicolaus Copernicus, published in 1512, that Earth was not the center of the solar system.

For more than 350 years, that was all anyone knew for certain about Venus. While the invention of bigger and better telescopes revealed ever more detail about the other planets in our solar system, they did not increase our knowledge of Venus. The problem was that Venus is entirely surrounded by a thick, opaque layer of clouds, so that all we can see from Earth is the top of this cloud cover. Through a telescope, Venus looks like a featureless, creamy ball. Astronomers were not even able to determine how long Venus's day was because, with no visible surface features as landmarks, there was no way to measure its rotation. Guesses ranged from 22 hours to 224 days.

The inability to see the surface of Venus did not stop astronomers from speculating about what might lie beneath its clouds. Knowing that Venus is a virtual twin of Earth in terms of size but that it orbits closer to the Sun, many scientists thought that Venus might be a world of primeval jungles, like Earth during the age of the dinosaurs. Some scientists deduced that since Venus was closer to the Sun than Earth, it would be warmer, and that its thick clouds would support a humid atmosphere with perhaps constant rain. Other astronomers suggested that Venus had no land at all and was covered instead by a worldwide ocean. Still others argued that the planet was a desert, dry and lifeless, eroded by powerful winds and baking under a temperature as high as the boiling point of water.

Seen through a telescope, Venus presents a nearly featureless face, with only the faintest hints of streaks in its swirling clouds. For centuries astronomers could not tell if they were actually observing the surface of the planet.

Some nineteenth-century astronomers thought that Venus might be a desert world of rugged mountains and blowing dust like the depiction shown here.

Even before the first space probes were sent to Venus in the early 1980s, astronomers were able to discover a little about the surface of the planet by using radar, which easily penetrates the cloud cover. By bouncing radar signals off the surface, they were able to learn something of its nature. They discovered that Venus is a rugged world without large continental masses or oceans like Earth. The signals suggested huge mountains, craters, and perhaps even volcanoes. And the question of Venus's rotation was solved by radar measurements. Astronomers found that it rotates *backward* (or **retrograde**) compared with all the other planets. Earth and the rest of the planets in the solar system rotate from west to east (counterclockwise as seen from above their north poles), but Venus spins from east to west, or clockwise. And this spin is very slow— it takes Venus 243 days to make one rotation. Why Venus's rotation is retrograde is yet one more mystery about the planet. It was only when the space probes arrived that astronomers began to realize what a strange world Venus *really* is.

Besides Mars, Venus was one of the most popular planets in early science fiction. Because it was shrouded in clouds, almost any kind of world could be imagined underneath them. The two theories about the surface of Venus that appealed most to science-fiction writers were that it might be a tropical world much like that of prehistoric Earth (left), or that it might be covered by a worldwide ocean.

One of the first science-fiction stories to be set on Venus, *Journey to Venus* (1895), by Gustavus Pope, depicted it as populated by dinosaurs and other prehistoric monsters. In 1909, Garrett Serviss's *A Columbus of Space* described Venus as always keeping one face toward the Sun, so that it had one perpetually sunlit hot side and one cold dark side. In the 1930s, Stanley G. Weinbaum set several classic short stories on a tropical Venus. Isaac Asimov described an ocean-covered Venus in his novel *The Oceans of Venus* (1954). More recent science fiction, such as Pamela Sargent's *Venus of Dreams* (1986) and *Venus of Shadows* (1988), describe Venus as we now know it to exist and speculate on how it might be possible to transform it into an Earthlike world on which humans might be able to live.

The following is a description of the first landing on Venus, from Garrett P. Serviss's 1909 novel, *A Columbus of Space:*

Suddenly, with the slightest perceptible bump, we touched the soil, and the car came to rest. We had landed on Venus!

"It's unquestionably frightfully cold outside," said Edmund, "and we'll now put on these things."

He dragged out of one of his many lockers four suits of thick fur garments, and as many pairs of fur gloves, together with caps and shields for the face, leaving only narrow openings for the eyes. When we had got them on we looked like so many [Eskimo]. Finally Edmund handed each of us a pair of small automatic pistols, telling us to put them where they would be handy in our side pockets . . .

Our preparations being made, we opened the door. The air that rushed in almost hardened us into icicles!

"It won't hurt you," said Edmund in a whisper. "It can't be down to absolute zero on account of the dense atmosphere. You'll get used to it in a few minutes. Come on."

His whispering gave us a sense of imminent danger, but nevertheless we followed as he led the way straight toward the shaft of light. On nearing it we saw that it came out of an irregularly round hole in the ground. When we got nearer we were astonished to see rough steps which led down into the pit. The next instant we were frozen in our tracks! For a moment my heart stopped beating.

Standing on the steps, just below the level of the ground, and intently watching us, with eyes as big and luminous as moons, was a creature shaped like a man, but more savage than a gorilla!

CHAPTER TWO

THE BIOGRAPHY OF A PLANET

Venus, like Earth and the other planets of the solar system, was formed about 4.5 billion years ago, shortly after the Sun itself was born. The early Sun was surrounded by a vast cloud of dust and particles left over from its formation. This dust was made of a wide variety of substances, from **silicate** minerals to carbon compounds to water. Gradually, over millions of years, these particles began to clump together. The larger clumps grew rapidly as their increasing gravity caused them to gather up smaller ones. A few of these clumps soon grew to a few miles in width, then to hundreds of miles. Eventually, there were only a few giant clumps of material. These became the planets.

In the hot inner region of the young solar system, near the Sun, only metallic and silicate particles could exist. More volatile materials such as water ice would not remain solid. This is why Mercury, Venus, Earth, and Mars are rocky worlds, or **terrestrial planets**. The lower temperatures farther out allowed icy particles and particles rich in carbon to form. So in the outer solar system we have the **carbonaceous** asteroids and ice-rich planets such as Jupiter, Saturn, Uranus, and Neptune—the **gas giants**—and their moons.

(14)

MERCURY VENUS EARTH MARS JUPITER SATURN URANUS NEPTUNE PLUTO

A family portrait: the planets and moons of our solar system shown to the same scale as the Sun

To understand how Venus and Earth became so different, we ought to first look at how Earth evolved, since we know much more about our planet. Four and a half billion years ago Earth was almost entirely **molten**, and during this period the iron it contained slowly drained to the **core** of the planet (because iron is one of the heaviest elements that the early Earth had in abundance). This is why Earth today has so much iron in its core but relatively little in its outer crust, which is composed mainly of lighter elements and minerals, such as aluminum, oxygen, and calcium. Soon afterward, Earth's outer crust began to **differentiate**; that is, it divided into different kinds of material. The crust—the part of our planet that we walk on—is as thin, in proportion to the entire Earth, as the shell of an egg. This hard outer crust is called the **lithosphere**, from Greek words meaning "sphere of rock." It is about 30 miles (50 km) thick and 6 miles (10 km) thick beneath the oceans.

Beneath the lithosphere lies a deep layer called the **asthenosphere**. This layer is hot enough to be plastic but not hot enough to be actually molten. Below the asthenosphere is the semisolid **mesosphere**. The asthenosphere and the mesophere together form the **mantle**, which extends from 400 miles (644 km) beneath the surface to 1,796 miles (2,890 km) beneath. Below this is a molten outer core of liquid nickel and iron that goes down 3,200 miles (5,150 km), and below that is a solid nickel-iron core 1,500 miles (2,414 km) in diameter. It is in the mantle that all of the circulation deep within Earth takes place, as heat from the molten core causes the semisolid material in the mantle to churn slowly like cooking oatmeal. The hot rock moves gradually up toward the surface of Earth, where it cools and slowly sinks back down toward the core again. This circular movement is called **convection**.

As the convection currents in the mantle reach the crust, they spread out. This causes the crust to move with the currents, resulting in the crust being broken up into huge moving plates called **continents**. While these plates can be very wide—up to several thousand miles—they are also very thin, only 30 to 90 miles (50

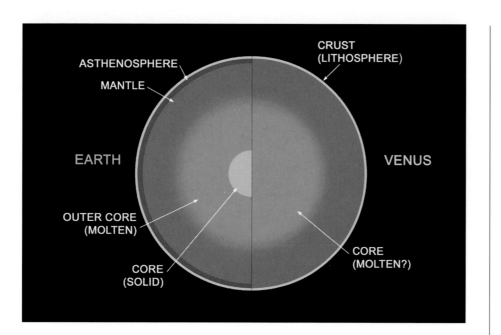

ASTHENOSPHERE

MANTLE

CRUST
(LITHOSPHERE)

EARTH

VENUS

OUTER CORE
(MOLTEN)

CORE
(SOLID)

CORE
(MOLTEN?)

Cross sections of Earth (left) and Venus (right): Venus is missing a solid core, as well as the asthenosphere, which makes the movement of crustal plates possible.

to 150 km) in thickness. They float on the semirigid asthenosphere like rafts on water.

The continental plates can collide—and when they do, huge mountain ranges, such as the Himalayas and Andes, can be created—and they can split apart, creating huge "rift valleys" such as the Atlantic Ocean, which was formed when North and South America split from Europe and Africa. When plates split apart, fresh molten material wells up from the mantle, creating fresh new crust, like a scab over a wound. Sometimes when plates collide, one continental plate will ride up over another one, forcing the other deep into the mantle, in a process called **subduction**, where it is melted and recycled. The process of continents moving around the surface of a planet is called **plate tectonics**. Much of the familiar landscape of Earth—its mountain ranges, coastlines, and ocean basins—is the result of our planet possessing continents that move around.

Unlike Earth, Venus never evolved continents—although scientists aren't entirely certain why. Without continents, Venus never experienced plate tectonics. One result of this is that its surface appears to be much the same over the whole planet. It might be said that instead of possessing the many continental plates of Earth, Venus's crust is one big, planet-wide plate. But why does Venus have no continents? After all, it resembles Earth in just about every other way. As with so many other differences between the two planets, the answer may have to do with water . . .

Or, in the case of Venus, the lack of water. On Earth, water is carried far beneath the surface when continental plates are subducted. This has resulted in the creation of the asthenosphere. This layer acts as a kind of resilient buffer between the hot, uprising mantle and the surface of the planet, causing the uprising movement to spread to the sides. This sideways movement powers the movement of the continental plates. It is believed that no asthenosphere was created on Venus because of the lack of large amounts of water. This means that uprising material from its mantle continues clear on up to the crust, where it creates huge mountains, highlands, and domes. The lack of water in Venus's crust has also caused the rocks and minerals it is composed of to be extremely hard and resistant to breaking, so that it is more difficult for Venus to form separate continental plates.

There are other mysteries about Venus. When the planet is between Earth and the Sun, the dark side of the planet is visible as a dim gray disk. Astronomers call this glow the "ashen light." What does this dim light come from? Sometimes when Earth's Moon is just a thin crescent in the sky, its dark side is visible as a faint gray circle. This is caused by earthlight shining on the Moon. But Venus has no moons, so it cannot be moonlight that is illuminating it. And it is not an optical illusion, as some have suggested.

It was once thought that the glow might be the light from vast forest fires sweeping across the planet, but we know now that is impossible since Venus has no life at all, let alone forests (or the oxygen needed to support combustion). Could there be some sort of chemical reaction in its strange atmosphere that is causing the glow? Could it have something to do with lightning? Or could it be an effect like Earth's auroras? To this day no one knows. It remains one of the mysteries of Venus.

ANOTHER VENUS MYSTERY

This overall, one-plate crust acts as a kind of "lid" that contains the heat beneath it, like the lid on a pot of boiling water. Without any way of escaping, the heat in the interior of the planet begins to increase, and convection currents become stronger. This eventually causes the lithosphere to break up, which results in a planetwide outbreak of volcanism, with an outpouring of **lava** that completely resurfaces the planet. The release of all of this heat causes the interior of Venus to cool again; then new, hard crust forms, and the cycle begins all over.

This is, however, only one theory to explain why Venus looks the way it does. There are many other theories, but no one really knows for certain why Venus evolved so differently from Earth. Until we get more information about the planet—its composition and how it was formed—we will not know for sure which theory is correct.

Facing page: No one knows for certain whether volcanic activity still occurs on Venus, but given the large number of volcanic features on the planet and its similarity to Earth, it is reasonable to suppose that there are still active volcanoes such as the one shown here.

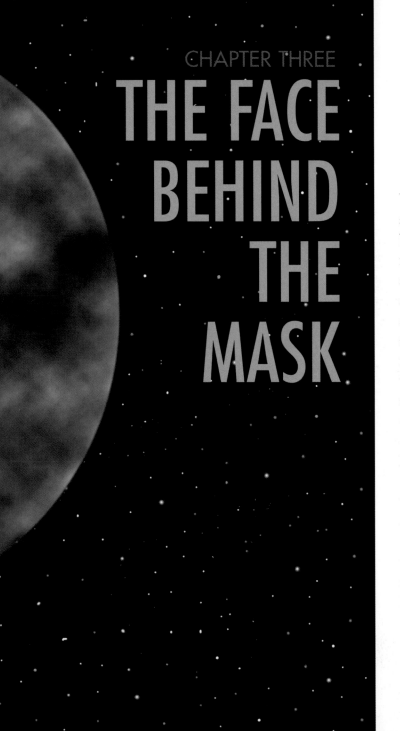

CHAPTER THREE

THE FACE BEHIND THE MASK

Venus's atmosphere was discovered in 1761 by a Russian astronomer named M. Lomonosov. Observing Venus as it passed between Earth and the Sun, he saw the backlit atmosphere illuminated in a ghostly ring around the planet. The nature of this atmosphere mystified scientists for two centuries, until astronomers at the Mount Wilson Observatory detected huge amounts of **carbon dioxide** (CO_2) using an instrument called a **spectrograph**. This allows astronomers to determine what elements exist on another planet by studying the light reflected from the planet itself. It was eventually determined that Venus's atmosphere is 96 percent carbon dioxide, which is the same gas you exhale when you breathe and the one that forms the bubbles in carbonated beverages. By comparison, only 0.00035 percent of Earth's atmosphere is carbon dioxide.

Very little more was learned about Venus until the 1960s, when information sent back to Earth by space probes allowed astronomers to calculate a surface temperature for Venus of about 891°F (477°C). This temperature is high enough to melt lead and tin. The finding certainly ruled out all the theories that Venus might be a tropical world like prehistoric Earth or that it might have huge oceans—those would have boiled away long ago.

Venus's atmosphere was discovered in 1761, when a Russian astronomer saw it illuminated as the planet passed in front of the Sun.

For centuries astronomers were prevented from seeing the surface (right) of Venus because of its heavy cloud cover (left). The surface was revealed by the *Magellan* orbiter, which was able to penetrate the clouds with its radar.

Scientists in the Soviet Union managed to land a probe on the surface of Venus in 1970. The probe confirmed the high temperature. It also measured an **atmospheric pressure** at the surface that is 90 times that of Earth's. Instead of the 14 pounds of air pressure per square inch we experience at the surface of our planet, a visitor on Venus would have to endure a pressure of 1,260 pounds on every square inch of his or her body—90 tons per square foot—the equivalent to being under 3,000 feet (914 meters) of water! Most submarines would be crushed by such pressure.

The density of Venus's atmosphere is only part of the reason for this tremendous pressure. The carbon dioxide of which it is composed is also important: CO_2 is a much heavier gas than the oxygen and nitrogen that compose the atmosphere of Earth. Since it weighs so much more than oxygen and nitrogen, it presses down more heavily on the surface of the planet.

The mystery of Venus's clouds was also solved in the early 1970s. It was discovered that instead of being composed of water droplets, like earthly clouds, they consist of tiny droplets of sulfuric acid. This is the same acid used in car batteries: a yellowish fluid that is very corrosive and can eat through most metals. The clouds are also very high above the surface: 30 to 36 miles (48 to 58 km), as opposed to the average cloud on Earth, which is less than 6 miles (10 km). Sulfuric acid rain probably falls from the clouds, but if so it never reaches the surface. It would evaporate in the high temperatures long before it got to the ground.

At an altitude of about 30 miles (50 km), the clouds of Venus are much higher than the highest clouds on Earth. Violent lightning discharges occur almost continuously. Above and below the cloud layer is a heavy haze of sulfuric acid. The temperature in the cloud deck is a moderate 56°F (13.3°C), even if the clouds themselves are poisonous and acidic. Fifteen miles (25 km) below this, however, the temperature rises to a searing 428°F (220°C), as hot as a kitchen oven set high. The acid rain that falls from the high clouds never reaches the surface—the temperature becomes so great that the acid evaporates before it falls more than 12 miles (20 km) or so. From this point down the atmosphere is cloudless.

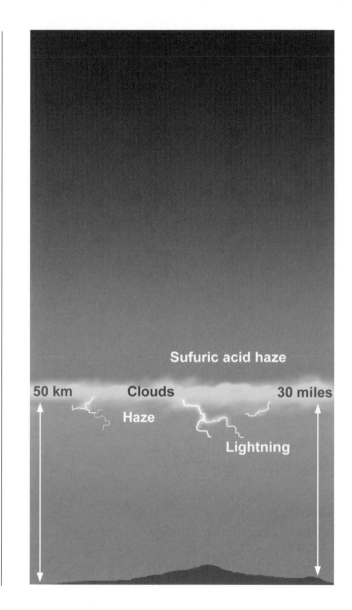

Sufuric acid haze

50 km   Clouds   30 miles

Haze

Lightning

In 1978, Russian and American probes discovered powerful bolts of lightning within the clouds. Beneath the cloud layer, the atmosphere seems to be clear. Instead of the gloomy, dark world imagined by many early science-fiction writers, the surface of Venus is as bright as Earth's surface on a lightly overcast day.

The classical symbol of love and beauty turned out to be a world of terrifying heat, acid rain, and crushing pressure. But *why* is Venus such a hostile planet? Why is it so hot? True, it is closer to the Sun than Earth is, but it is not so close that such high temperatures can be accounted for by that fact alone. The planet Mercury lies almost twice as close to the Sun as Venus does, yet its surface is nowhere near as hot. The answer is in Venus's dense atmosphere.

In the case of an airless planet, such as Mercury, the heat the surface receives from the Sun is radiated back out into space. But if the planet has an atmosphere, like Venus and Earth, the situation changes. An atmosphere traps much of the incoming solar radiation, keeping it from radiating back out into space, so the temperature at the surface can become very high. This kind of heating is called the **greenhouse effect**. The glass panes of a greenhouse allow the **infrared radiation** of sunlight to penetrate, but prevent the heat being radiated by the surfaces inside the greenhouse from escaping. This is because the infrared radiation from the Sun is much more energetic, or powerful, than the heat radiated by warm soil. The lower-energy heat cannot get back out through the glass. This allows the temperature inside the greenhouse to become greater than the temperature outside.

When sunlight reaches the surface of Earth, the surface warms up. The warm surface then radiates heat in the form of infrared radiation. If Earth were airless, this heat would simply radiate back out into space. But the outgoing infrared is not as powerful as the original sunlight and cannot as easily penetrate the atmosphere. This heat is trapped and causes Earth to gradually become warmer.

Two gases are particularly good at trapping infrared radiation: water vapor and carbon dioxide. For this reason they are called **greenhouse gases**. Fortunately for life on our world, Earth has just enough of these gases to keep it pleasantly warm, but not so much as to make it too hot for life to exist. But if the amount of greenhouse gases were to increase, the average temperature of Earth would increase. Already the average temperature of our planet has risen in the last century. There is a lot of debate about the cause of this "global warming," but there seems to be a clear link with our increased use of fossil fuels, which produce CO_2 when they burn.

Powerful infrared radiation from the Sun penetrates Earth's atmosphere and heats the surface.

Infrared radiation from the surface is too weak to penetrate the atmosphere.

Since more heat comes in than escapes, the surface gets hotter and hotter.

GREENHOUSE EFFECT EXPERIMENT

You will need: a large glass jar that holds at least one quart (1 liter) with a lid, dirt, and two thermometers.

Turn the jar on its side and put enough dirt in it to fill it level with the mouth. Place one of the thermometers face up on the dirt and put on the lid. Lay the jar on its side where sunlight can shine directly on it. Place the other thermometer in the sunlight alongside the jar. Wait for about an hour and compare the temperatures. Which thermometer reads higher? The one inside the jar will be registering a much higher temperature. The reason is that light from the Sun can pass easily through the glass, where it then warms up the dirt. The heat energy from the dirt, however, is not as strong as that from the Sun, so it cannot pass back through the glass. Instead, it is trapped inside the jar. Since more energy is coming in than is escaping, the inside of the jar grows hotter than the outside air. In this experiment, the glass acts like the atmosphere of Earth or Venus.

The carbon dioxide (and to some extent water vapor and other gases) in Earth's atmosphere acts like the glass panes in a greenhouse. High-energy radiation from the Sun easily penetrates the atmosphere and heats up the surface. This warm surface radiates heat in the form of infrared radiation, but it is too weak to escape back out into space. The atmosphere acts like a one-way road: It is easier for solar radiation to get in than it is for infrared radiation to get out. Fortunately for us, there is not enough CO_2 in Earth's atmosphere to keep in all of the heat, and most of it does manage to escape. (It is as though there are some panes missing in the roof of the greenhouse.) Venus's atmosphere, however, is almost entirely CO_2, so most of the heat the planet receives from the Sun is trapped beneath the clouds, unable to escape.

But *how* did Venus gather so much CO_2? Since it resembles Earth in every other way, why is its atmosphere so different? Astronomer William Hartmann thinks it would be more interesting to ask why Earth does *not* have an atmosphere of CO_2.

Much of Earth's early atmosphere was created by gases emitted by volcanoes. These gases were mostly water vapor and CO_2. The water vapor formed our oceans, and the CO_2 was dissolved in the water. Animals such as **diatoms** used this CO_2 in creating their shells, which are made of substances called **carbonates**. Over billions of years, these shells eventually formed vast beds of carbonate rocks, such as chalk and limestone. Most of Earth's original carbon dioxide is now contained in these beds.

Like Earth, the early atmosphere of Venus was probably mostly carbon dioxide. Venus also might have had oceans, but it may not

Facing page: Early in the history of Venus, volcanoes poured vast quantities of carbon dioxide into the atmosphere.

have had as much water as Earth, so these short-lived oceans may never have been very large. Since Venus is closer to the Sun, these shallow oceans would have quickly evaporated. If there were no large permanent oceans to absorb CO_2, the gas would have had nowhere else to go but the atmosphere. Amazingly enough, it has been shown that Earth and Venus have the same amounts of CO_2—Earth's is safely stored in its oceans and carbonaceous rocks, while Venus's is loose in its atmosphere.

Things may be changing for Earth, however. Increased levels of carbon dioxide in the atmosphere, mainly from burning fossil fuels, has caused an increase in the average temperature of our planet. What we have learned from Venus is an excellent example of how we can learn more about our planet by studying other ones.

Facing page: Venus may have had many shallow oceans, such as the one shown here. Long before the oceans were able to absorb much of the carbon dioxide being spewed from volcanoes—as the oceans on Earth did—they evaporated. Without large oceans to soak up excess CO_2, Venus's atmosphere soon became filled with the gas. This was the beginning of the extreme greenhouse effect that caused Venus to become the hottest planet in the solar system.

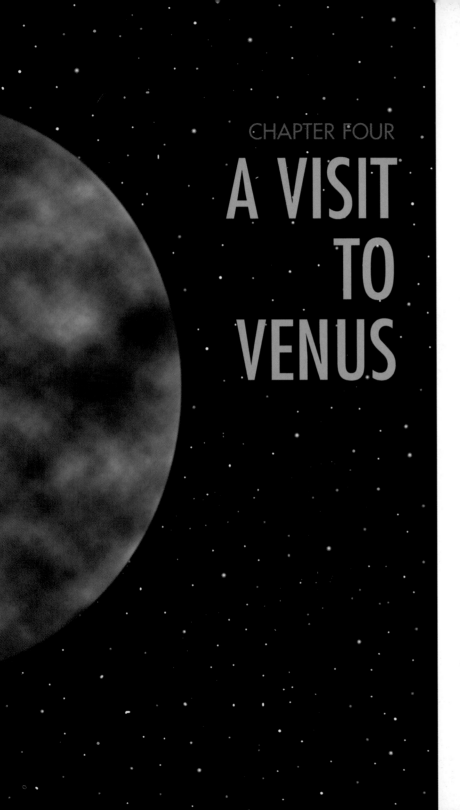

CHAPTER FOUR

A VISIT TO VENUS

Spacecraft sent to Venus between 1975 and 1990 have given us a very clear idea of what kind of landscape lies beneath the blanket of clouds. The first of these, the Soviet Union's *Venera* landers, actually managed to set down on the surface of the planet. Before they were destroyed by the hostile environment, which took only about 15 minutes, they managed to send back a handful of photos; they showed a barren volcanic landscape covered with flat, sharp-edged rocks. Even though the sky was completely cloud-covered, the lighting was very bright—about what one would see on an overcast summer day on Earth. Many astronomers had thought that the cloud cover might be too dense to allow much sunlight through and that the surface of Venus would be dark.

Almost the entire surface of Venus has been mapped in detail by Soviet and American orbiters, such as *Pioneer*, *Venera*, and especially *Magellan*. By using radar bounced from the surface it is possible to tell what the terrain is like, whether it is rough or smooth, high or low. These probes discovered that the differences between Venus and Earth may be even greater than anyone previously suspected. For one thing, if we could see Venus without its clouds, it would *look* very different from Earth.

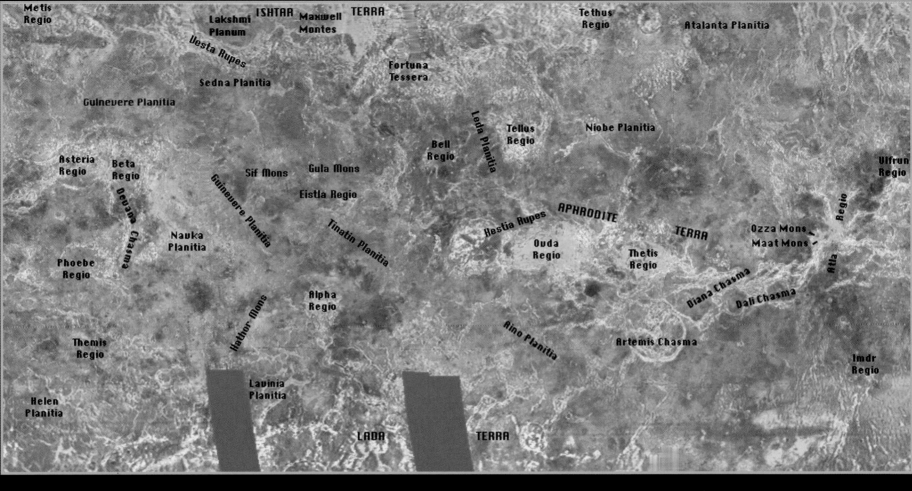

Metis Regio

Lakshmi Planum ISHTAR Maxwell Montes TERRA

Tethus Regio Atalanta Planitia

Vesta Rupes

Fortuna Tessera

Sedna Planitia

Gulnevere Planitia

Leda Planitia Tellus Regio Niobe Planitia

Bell Regio

Asteria Regio Beta Regio Sif Mons Gula Mons

Ulfrun Regio

Devana Chasma Guinevere Planitia Eistla Regio

Hestia Rupes APHRODITE

TERRA Ozza Mons Maat Mons Regio

Nauka Planitia Tinatin Planitia Ouda Regio Thetis Regio Atla Regio

Phoebe Regio Diana Chasma Dali Chasma

Hathor Mons Alpha Regio

Themis Regio Rino Planitia Artemis Chasma Imdr Regio

Helen Planitia Lavinia Planitia

LADA TERRA

On this map of Venus, the colors indicate the height of various regions (they do not represent the true colors of Venus). The orange areas are the highest (the small red spot of Maxwell Montes in the north is the highest on the planet), and the light purple areas are the lowest. NASA did not receive data for the area showing gray boxes at the bottom. (NASA/JPL)

A typical landscape on Venus: flat plains covered with sharp, volcanic rocks with occasional steep mountains and plateaus. If there is still active volcanism on the planet there may be **fumaroles**, or vents, such as the one in the left foreground, surrounded by colorful mineral deposits.

Unlike our planet, with its distinct continental masses, Venus's surface is dominated by vast, gently rolling plains and lowlands. Venus's flat terrain and lack of large continental masses suggest that it has experienced little or no continental drift, where large continental "plates" collide with one another, creating large folded mountain ranges like the Andes and Himalayas. Mountains and highlands cover only about 15 or 20 percent of the planet. These highlands are Australia-sized plateaus that superficially resemble the continents of Earth. Parts of these highland areas are huge volcanoes rising up to 35,000 feet (10,668 m) above the surrounding plains, which is higher than Mount Everest, the tallest mountain on Earth at 29,035 feet (8,850 m).

Venus has a large number of giant impact craters, about a thousand of them, some up to 124 miles (200 km) wide. There are very few craters smaller than 1.25 miles (2 km). This lack of small craters is due to Venus's extraordinarily thick atmosphere: Small **meteoroids** are simply shattered into powder long before they can reach the ground. Only the largest objects possess enough mass and energy to hit the surface.

Venus's craters also seem to be scattered evenly over its entire surface. Earth, the Moon, and Mars, for instance, all have ancient highly cratered regions mixed with younger lightly cratered regions. In contrast, the surface of Venus seems to be about the same age everywhere, and relatively young at that. Using the cratering on the Moon as a guide, it would seem that none of Venus's surface could be much older than about 500 million years. This might seem to be very old, but it is only about 10 percent of

Venus's 5 billion-year history. There are places on Earth's surface that are as old as 3.9 billion years—eight times older than any place on Venus. Why the surface of Venus appears to be so young is a great puzzle for scientists.

One possibility is that the volcanoes might destroy meteor craters almost as fast as they are formed. This would mean that the number of craters we see at any one time remains fairly constant. It would also explain why most of the craters seem so young. Another idea is that about 500 million years ago, a vast volcanic

Venus's dense atmosphere causes most meteors to burn up long before they reach the ground. But if one is large enough—a small asteroid, perhaps—it can survive and blow a huge crater out of the landscape. This is why the few craters on Venus are mostly very large ones. Here the view is from the brink of one of these enormous craters, with the opposite rim miles away. In the front is a smaller crater, created by a meteor just barely large enough to reach the surface.

The older the surface of a moon or planet is, the more craters it will have. Even though most of Earth's ancient craters have been erased by erosion and the movement of its continental plates, it is still possible to find the scars of these impacts. They show that Earth has been hit as many times as Venus. The largest craters on Earth are also usually the oldest craters, since there were far more large objects wandering around in our solar system when it was younger than there are today. Most of these large objects were long ago swept up by the planets, so that today most meteoroids are fairly small. The puzzle about Venus is that its large, ancient craters seem to be so well preserved. Even though Venus has no rain and little or no **tectonic** activity, scientists would have expected the oldest craters to be destroyed by the many immense lava flows. By comparison, typical surfaces on Earth are only 100 million years old, though some places in Canada go as far back as 3.9 billion years, while the surface of the Moon ranges from 3 to 4.5 billion years old.

The surface age of a planet can be much younger than the planet itself because planetary surfaces are constantly undergoing changes. Meteoroid impacts, volcanic activity, tectonic forces, erosion, and weather all have the effect of reshaping and even replacing the original surface. For this reason the surface we see may be much newer than the planet itself.

eruption covered the entire planet with lava, wiping out all of Venus's ancient craters. If this happened, then all of the craters we see today have been formed since then.

Almost all of Venus's meteor craters are very fresh-looking because of the absence of erosion. It does not rain on Venus, and the winds are too slow to wear down the landscape very much. Any changes to the landscape more likely are due to the extreme heat. Some craters are odd-looking, resembling large, dark blotches rather than the circular holes we would normally expect. This might be the result of large meteorites exploding before they hit the ground. The resulting shock wave would then have shattered the surface below. Sometimes these splotches have a collection of small, irregularly shaped craters in the middle, suggesting that the meteorite may have broken up into many pieces before impacting. The dark, smooth areas that surround these features might be a blanket of dust and ash that fell from the exploding meteorite.

The orbiters discovered many other strange features on Venus, such as enormous bull's-eye-shaped regions called **coronas**. Ranging from 130 to 1,300 miles (200 to 2,000 km) across, they probably were formed by molten rock, or **magma**, lifting the surface from below like a giant bubble, which then sagged and cracked as the magma flowed out from beneath it. Since the surface of Venus is so hot, most of the rocks in its crust are already only a few hundred degrees short of melting temperature. Rocks this hot would bend like taffy if enough pressure were put on them. This makes it easy for volcanic heat to distort the surface, or even to melt it altogether.

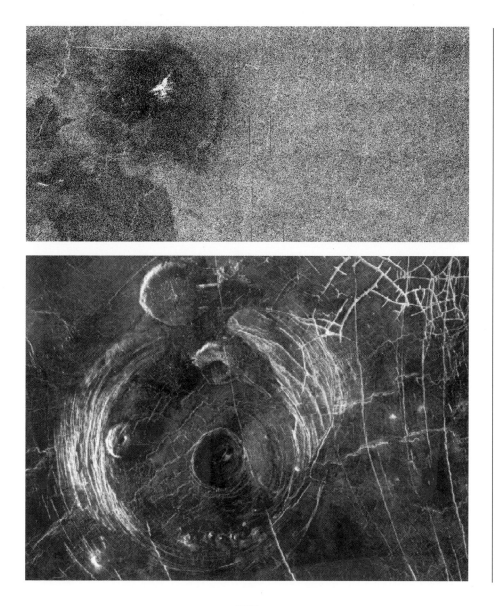

A "shadow crater" in the Lakshmi Region is shown here: Venus's dense atmosphere prevents all but the very largest meteors from reaching the surface. Many explode in the air before hitting the ground, covering the surface below with a circular patch of ash and debris. A few small remnants of this meteor managed to hit, creating the little impacts in the center of the "shadow." (NASA/JPL)

This *Magellan* radar image shows an area in a plain southwest of Aphrodite Terra. The large feature in the center is Aine Corona, a circular pattern of fractures 120 miles (200 km) in diameter. Just north of Aine Corona is a low, flat-topped volcano. It is about 21 miles (35 km) in diameter. At the upper right of the image is a complex pattern of fractures caused when magma drains from beneath the surface and the overlying crust collapses. (NASA/JPL)

In keeping with Venus's traditional association with love and beauty, most of its features are named after famous women from history or mythology. Included are great artists, poets, scientists, explorers, doctors, and humanitarians, as well as queens, warriors, and goddesses from every nationality and culture on Earth. Among the thousands of women whose names were used for features of Venus are Louisa May Alcott, author of *Little Women*; Mary Cassatt, the great Impressionist painter; Margaret Bourke-White, the pioneer news photographer; Clara Barton, founder of the Red Cross; Sacagawea; Pocahontas; Helen Keller; Harriet Tubman; Bathsheba, the mother of King Solomon; and Cleopatra. The lone male for whom a feature of Venus was named is James Clerk Maxwell, a nineteenth-century British physicist. He is honored for his research leading to the invention of radar, which has been so important in the exploration of Venus.

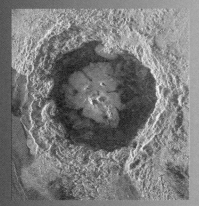

This large crater is named after the poet Emily Dickinson. It is 45 miles (69 km) wide. Its dark, smooth floor is probably lava that filled the crater after it was formed. (NASA/JPL)

Venus is distinguished by its large number of volcanoes. The giant volcanoes of Venus are surrounded by immense lava flows that extend for hundreds of miles. These flows are fractured and broken and covered with vast ridges, probably caused by the ground beneath collapsing under the weight of lava thousands of feet thick. Though no one knows for sure, it is possible that many of these volcanoes are still active.

Most of Venus's plains lie in the lowest areas of the planet, just where one would expect lava to pool, like water filling the great ocean basins of Earth. These broad lava plains cover 85 percent of Venus. Snaking through them are sinuous channels, called **rills**, that may have been created by flowing lava, like water in a riverbed. The longest of these channels, Baltis Vallis, is 4,225 miles (6,800 km) long, longer than the Amazon or Nile, Earth's longest rivers.

The great lava plains are not perfectly flat or featureless. In addition to the rills there are regions where the surface has wrinkled into long, narrow, parallel ridges. There are also broad **ridge belts** rising a few hundred feet above the surrounding surface. They consist of hundreds of smaller, intertwined ridges and can be hundreds of miles long but only a few miles wide. Both of these features—the wrinkle ridges and ridge belts—were probably the result of stresses the lava plain underwent while it was cooling, causing it to deform in much the same way an apple or other fruit will wrinkle as it dries.

Most of Venus's volcanoes are small **shield volcanoes** less than 12.5 miles (20 km) in diameter. Shield volcanoes form when lava flows evenly from a vent in the surface, gradually building up a wide, low mound. Hawaii's volcanoes are examples of shield vol-

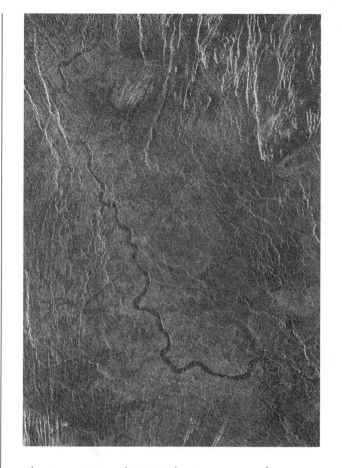

This photograph shows small volcanic domes on the slopes of the Maat volcano in East Ovda. The central one is probably only about 2,257 feet (688 m) high. The bright area to the east is most likely an old lava flow. The image covers an area 56 miles (90 km) wide. (NASA/JPL)

This is a 124-mile (200-km) segment of a channel that winds across the surface of Venus. Though such channels resemble rivers, they were probably created by flowing lava rather than by water. (NASA/JPL)

Some regions of Venus's landscape are broken up by deep rills, or winding valleys. Some of these may have been created by flowing lava, while others may be cracks caused by movement of magma beneath the surface.

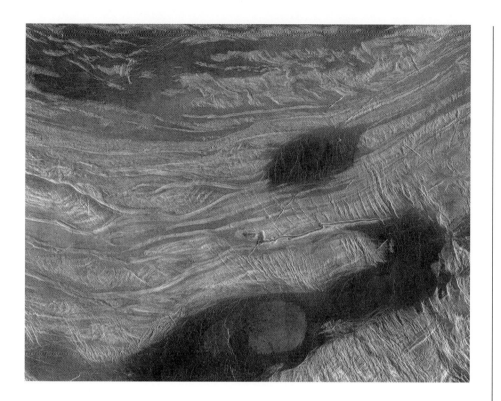

Ovda Regio is a large highland near the equator. It is covered with hundreds of ridges 5 to 9 miles (8 to 15 km) wide and 20 to 40 miles (30 to 60 km) long, which formed when the crust of the planet wrinkled. Some of the ridges are cut by deep fractures. The areas between the ridges are filled with dark material, either lava or windblown soil. (NASA/JPL)

canoes on Earth, while Olympus Mons, on Mars, is the largest shield volcano in the solar system.

Some of Venus's larger shield volcanoes resemble enormous flat pancakes 12.5 to 60 miles (20 to 100 km) wide. These were formed by very **viscous**, or thick, lava flowing slowly over the surface, just as pancake batter makes a round flat disk when poured into a skillet. The largest of Venus's volcanoes resemble the big volcanoes of Earth. These are at least 60 miles (100 km) across. Sapas Mons, a

A few of Venus's strange "pancake" volcanoes are visible here. They were formed when very thick lava oozed slowly from a vent in the surface, spreading like thick syrup poured onto a tabletop. The largest one shown here is 39 miles (65 km) wide and only 0.6 mile (1 km) high. (NASA/JPL)

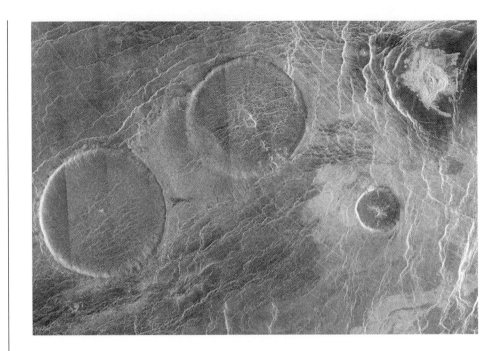

typical shield volcano, is 248 miles (400 km) wide at the base and nearly 5,000 feet (1.5 km) high. The lava that poured from it flowed for hundreds of miles over the surrounding landscape.

The remainder of Venus is covered by its highlands, only about 15 percent of its surface. Unlike the smooth, rolling lava plains, the highlands tend to be very rough territory, with many mountains, volcanoes, ridges, fractures, and canyons. There are several highland regions, but the two largest—the closest Venus has to real "continents"—are Aphrodite Terra, which lies on the equator, and Ishtar Terra, which lies in the far north. Aphrodite is distin-

In the high peaks of Venus's mountains

Aphrodite Terra has numerous large canyons. Diana Chasma and Dali Chasma are near the east end of the continent. The walls of the larger of the two canyons, Dali Chasma, can rise as high as 3.7 miles (6 km) above the rugged canyon floor.

guished by a pair of canyons, Diana Chasma and Dali Chasma. These canyons were caused when the crust split and pulled apart, like the Great Rift Valley of Africa or the Mid-Atlantic Ridge of the Atlantic Ocean.

Ishtar Terra in the north boasts rugged mountain ranges. Especially impressive is one called Maxwell Montes, with its steep slopes (up to 35 degrees) and extreme height of 7 miles (12 km), 2 miles higher than Mount Everest. These features suggest that Maxwell Montes may be a very young formation, not worn down by time like older mountains.

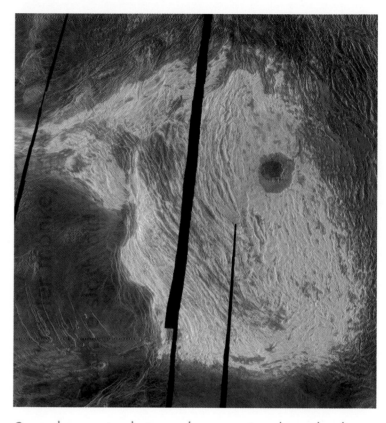

Several separate photographs were pieced together by NASA to make this full image of Maxwell Montes, the light-colored area in this picture. They lie in the far northern regions of Venus and are the highest mountains on the planet, 6.8 miles (11 km) higher than the average elevation of the plains. They are very rugged, with steep sides. To the east is the crater Cleopatra, a fairly young impact 62 miles (100 km) wide. There were no photographs available to fill in the three missing black areas of this image. (NASA/JPL)

Maxwell Montes.

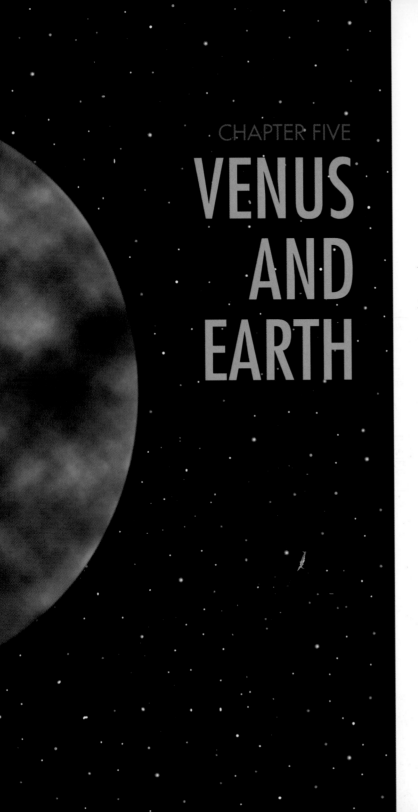

CHAPTER FIVE

VENUS AND EARTH

Why is Venus so different from Earth? Common sense would suggest that the two planets ought to be very much alike. After all, Venus is nearly a twin of our planet: It is made of the same elements, was formed at the same time, is nearly the same size, and lies only 30 percent closer to the Sun than Earth does. Yet it is radically different. Instead of wondering why Venus is so different from Earth, it might be worth asking another question: Why isn't Earth more like Venus? Perhaps it is Earth that is out of step.

One of the most important features of our planet that sets it apart from all others in the solar system is the existence of liquid water on its surface. Earth has so much water—three-fourths of its surface is covered with it—that it has more than once been suggested that it has been misnamed: Our planet should be called "Ocean" instead of "Earth." Our oceans absorbed most of the carbon dioxide from the early atmosphere, preventing the runaway greenhouse effect that turned Venus into an inferno. The lack of water on Venus may also help account for the way its surface has been shaped.

On Earth, water is a major component in the creation of the different types of rock that compose the planet's crust. Some of these rocks are lighter than others, such as the rock that composes the continents, and will "float" on top of the heavier rock below. This differentiation means that Earth's crust is able to circulate laterally—that is, the continental plates slide over the surface like giant rafts, colliding with each other and occasionally passing over or under each other. When the latter happens, the crust that ends up at the bottom is melted down and recycled. On Venus, however, the lack of water means that its rocks are more or less all one type. This material circulates vertically, like cooking oatmeal. Molten rock rises from below, causing the great volcanoes and other volcanic features, while cooler, heavier rock sinks. There it is then remelted and rises back to the surface again.

The crusts of Earth (left) and Venus (right): Earth's convection currents are insulated from the outer crust by the asthenosphere. This causes the outer crust to be carried along by the currents, creating mountains and ridges. Since the convection currents in Venus's mantle rise much closer to the outer crust, they have a tendency to create stationary "hot spots," as well as areas where the crust is piled up into domes.

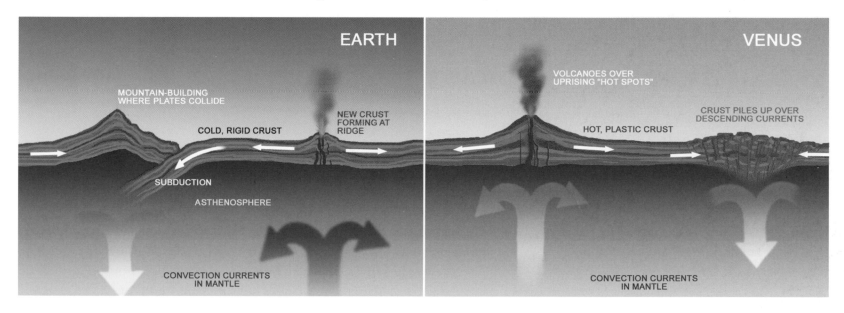

EARTH

MOUNTAIN-BUILDING
WHERE PLATES COLLIDE

COLD, RIGID CRUST

NEW CRUST
FORMING AT
RIDGE

SUBDUCTION

ASTHENOSPHERE

CONVECTION CURRENTS
IN MANTLE

VENUS

VOLCANOES OVER
UPRISING "HOT SPOTS"

CRUST PILES UP OVER
DESCENDING CURRENTS

HOT, PLASTIC CRUST

CONVECTION CURRENTS
IN MANTLE

OBSERVING VENUS

Venus is often visible in either the morning or evening sky, just before sunrise or just after sunset. Magazines such as *Astronomy* or *Sky & Telescope* can tell you when Venus can be seen during each month. When it is visible, it is one of the brightest stars in the sky. It is easy to see its shape with a pair of good binoculars, though a telescope is even better.

Is there any possibility that Earth could someday be like Venus? The answer is a frightening one: Yes, it's possible. The main elements that set Venus apart from Earth are Venus's incredible surface temperature and unbreathable atmosphere. If it were not for these the planet would be a very Earthlike world. Greenhouse gases are responsible for the difference.

Venus's atmosphere is composed of almost nothing but CO_2, an excellent greenhouse gas, while Earth has very little CO_2 in its atmosphere. But the amount of CO_2 in Earth's atmosphere appears to be increasing. Some of this comes from natural sources, such as volcanoes, but some of it also comes from the burning of fossil fuels, such as oil and gasoline. This is worsened by the destruction of forests, which would absorb CO_2 and produce oxygen. None of these would actually produce the amount of CO_2 that Venus possesses, but it would take only a fraction of that amount to cause a greenhouse effect that would make life impossible on Earth.

There have been many debates about the causes of the present global warming of Earth. It may be due to increased burning of fossil fuels, or it may be a natural cycle Earth goes through. Few scientists, however, doubt that Earth is growing warmer. Measurements made in the 1990s showed the highest average global temperature in more than a century. Although these changes seem small—the average increase is only a few degrees— the effects could be devastating. All of the systems that make our world what it is—its weather, oceans, forests, and hundreds of other factors—work together in a complex symphony that is as delicately balanced as a fine watch. It would take only a very small disturbance to any one part of this order to bring the whole thing

The eruption of a large volcano pours even more greenhouse gases into Venus's atmosphere.

down. The result could be a very different world from the one we now know—and it might not be one we could live on.

What will happen as Earth grows warmer? Thousands of square miles of farmland will be lost as deserts expand. Sea levels will rise as ice on the Antarctic ice cap melts. Populated sea-level regions from Florida to Bangladesh will be severely affected by even a small change in ocean levels. An increase of just a few degrees in the average temperature of seawater will kill hundreds of species of sea life—and hundreds more that depend on those for food will die.

Venus—and Jupiter and Mars and all the other worlds we share our solar system with—has something to teach us about how Earth works. By studying how and why these planets resemble our own, and how and why they are different, we gain deeper insight into the origins of Earth, how it works, and what its future may be.

CHAPTER SIX

EXPLORING VENUS

Venus is one of the most-explored planets in the solar system, having been visited by more than two dozen space probes. The U.S. space probe *Mariner 2* flew by the planet in 1962, the first to visit. Coming within 21,640 miles (34,830 km), the probe looked for radiation belts and magnetic fields, but found none, and took measurements of the temperature and atmospheric surface pressure. Two more Mariner flybys were made, in 1967 and 1973. During the latter mission, the first close-up pictures were taken of Venus.

The Soviet Union, meanwhile, launched several probes, beginning with *Venera 1* in 1961. In 1964 the Soviets were able to successfully drop an instrument package into the atmosphere, and this confirmed that Venus is made up almost entirely of carbon dioxide. *Venera 7* was the first spacecraft to actually land on Venus, in 1970, and it managed to send back information for a few minutes before being destroyed by the pressure and heat. A later lander, *Venera 10*, sent back the first pictures from the surface before it, too, was destroyed by the environment. So far no one has been able to build a spacecraft strong enough to resist the incredibly harsh conditions that exist on Venus.

EXPLORING VENUS

PROBE	DATE	MISSION
Mariner 2	August 27, 1962	Flyby of Venus; found dense atmosphere and hot surface
Venera 4	June 12, 1967	First atmosphere entry; came to within 15.5 mi (25 km) of surface
Mariner 5	June 14, 1967	Flyby
Venera 7	August 17, 1970	First spacecraft to successfully land on surface
Venera 8	March 27, 1972	Atmosphere probe
Venera 9	June 8, 1975	Orbiter and lander; first photos of surface
Venera 10	June 14, 1975	Orbiter and lander; sent photos from surface
Pioneer–Venus 1	May 20, 1978	Orbiter; sent photos of planet from space
Pioneer–Venus 2	August 8, 1978	Sent four probes into atmosphere
Venera 11	September 9, 1978	Flyby and lander
Venera 12	September 14, 1978	Flyby and lander
Venera 13	October 30, 1981	Flyby and lander; first color photos of surface
Venera 14	November 4, 1981	Flyby and lander; color photos of surface
Venera 15	June 2, 1983	Orbiter; radar mapped surface
Venera 16	June 7, 1983	Orbiter; radar mapped surface
Vega 1	December 15, 1984	Lander and balloon atmosphere probe
Vega 2	December 21, 1984	Lander and balloon atmosphere probe
Magellan	May 4, 1989	Orbiter; radar mapped surface

This 10.8-mile (17.4-km) -diameter volcanic dome imaged by *Magellan*'s radar has collapsed on its northwest and northeast slopes, resulting in landslides that have caused material to flow onto the surrounding plain. (NASA/JPL)

The *Venera 14* lander took this image of the surface of Venus. It reveals slabs of lava and gravelly soil. The picture was made from two different photos (accounting for the slight difference in color between the right and left halves.) The curvature is caused by the camera's wide-angle lens, and the elements on the bottom of the photo are parts of the spacecraft. (NASA/JPL)

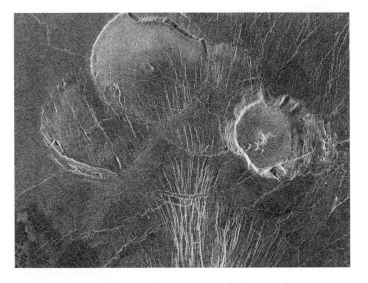

This is a *Magellan* radar image of three volcanoes in the Guinevere Planitia lowlands. The one in the center is a large, flat mound 31 miles (50 km) wide, which probably formed when thick, viscous lava flowed onto the surface. Surrounding the rim of the volcano is a steep scarp, or cliff, probably caused when the edge of the flow collapsed. This volcano lies partly atop another one to the southwest. The volcano to the east, which is 15.5 miles (25 km) in diameter, is probably the highest of the three. It, too, has steep cliffs around its edge. (NASA/JPL)

The Soviet Union was also the first to send spacecraft into orbit around Venus, which enabled long-term observations to be made. In 1984 the Soviets sent two *Vega* spacecraft to Venus, where they released a pair of French-built probes into the atmosphere. These floated beneath balloons, sending back valuable information about the composition, temperatures, and winds of the upper atmosphere.

One of the most successful missions to Venus has been that of the U.S. *Magellan* orbiter, which has created a detailed radar map of nearly the entire surface of the planet. Radar reflected from the surface can detect subtle differences in altitude and roughness. This allows scientists not only to detect mountains and valleys, but also to determine something about conditions on the surface. Its smoothness or roughness yields information about the kinds of lava that might be there.

Will human beings ever explore Venus? This seems highly unlikely. The conditions on the surface are extraordinarily hostile—most probes that have reached the surface have been destroyed within a few minutes. A lander with people on board would have to withstand the crushing pressure, furnacelike heat, and acid rain—and if the astronauts wanted to leave their spacecraft they would need rovers and spacesuits capable of dealing with these incredibly harsh conditions. But history has shown that human curiosity is a powerful force. People have usually figured out a way to go anyplace they want.

asthenosphere: a layer just beneath the crust of a planet. The rock in the asthenosphere is not hot enough to be completely molten. It acts as a kind of buffer between the outer crust and the convection currents in the molten mantle.

atmospheric pressure: the weight of a planet's atmosphere on the surface.

carbonaceous: describes minerals containing carbon.

carbonates: minerals containing carbon dioxide, such as chalk and limestone.

carbon dioxide: a heavy, colorless, odorless gas. Its chemical symbol is CO_2. It is one of the products of combustion, such as burning fossil fuels or breathing.

chasma: a canyon.

continent: a mass of light rock "floating" on top of a layer of heavier rock.

convection: the distribution of heat by the movement of the heated substance. This often results in a circulatory movement, such as that observed in cooking oatmeal.

core: the center of a planet. The cores of some planets are molten, while those of others are solid.

corona: a large circular formation of cracks and ridges created when a lava dome partially collapses.

diatom: a microscopic, one-celled plant that forms a protective skeleton of silica.

differentiation: the process by which different minerals and elements in a planet are separated into layers.

fumarole: a small, volcanic vent that releases steam and other gases.

gas giant: a large planet made mostly of gas and liquid, usually with a small rocky core.

greenhouse effect: an occurrence when atmospheric

gases prevent heat from escaping a planet.

greenhouse gases: gases that prevent the escape of infrared radiation from the surface of a planet—for example, carbon dioxide and water vapor.

infrared radiation: radiation beyond the red end of the visible spectrum; although we cannot see it, we feel infrared as heat.

lava: molten rock when it flows onto a surface (*also see* magma).

lithosphere: the outer, rocky surface of a terrestrial planet.

magma: molten rock while still underground (*also see* lava).

mantle: a semiliquid layer of rock that lies between the core and outer crust of a planet's interior.

mesosphere: the lower part of the asthenosphere; together they form the mantle.

meteoroid: a small rocky or metallic body in space—called a *meteor* when it enters the atmosphere and creates a streak of light due to friction; called a *meteorite* when found on the surface of Earth.

molten: the state of being liquid. When rock or metal becomes hot enough to melt, it is said to be molten.

Montes: mountains.

phases: the effect of sunlight illuminating a planet or moon.

planum: plains.

plate tectonics: the motion of continental masses on the surface of a planet.

retrograde: rotation from east to west, or clockwise, when looking down on the North Pole. Counterclockwise rotation is called *prograde*.

ridge belts: regions of parallel ridges.

rills: long, narrow, meandering valleys.

shield volcano: a low, mound-shaped volcano created by a steady flow of lava.

silica: silicon dioxide—of which ordinary sand is mostly made.

silicate: a mineral that contains silica.

spectrograph: a photograph of a spectrum, usually produced by an instrument called a *spectroscope*, which allows scientists to determine what elements are present on a star or planet.

subduction: an occurrence when one continental plate is forced beneath another.

tectonic: relating to the movement of continental masses, or "plates," on a planet.

terra: a large landmass similar to a continent on Earth.

terrestrial planet: a planet composed mostly of rocks and metals, such as Earth, Venus, or Mars.

viscous: fluid with a syruplike consistency.

Books

Beatty, J. Kelly, Carolyn Collins Petersen, and Andrew Chaikin, eds. *The New Solar System*. Cambridge, MA: Sky Publishing Corp, 1999.

Hartmann, William K. *Moons and Planets*. Belmont, CA: Wadsworth Publishing Co., 1999.

Kallen, Stuart A. *Exploring the Origins of the Universe*. Brookfield, CT: Twenty-First Century Books, 1997.

Miller, Ron, and William K. Hartmann. *The Grand Tour*. New York: Workman Publishing Co., 1993.

Scagell, Robine. *The New Book of Space*. Brookfield, CT: Copper Beech, 1997.

Schaaf, Fred. *Planetology*. Danbury, CT: Franklin Watts, 1996.

Spangenburg, Ray, and Kit Moser. *Artificial Satellites*. Danbury, CT: Franklin Watts, 2001.

———. *A Look at Venus*. Danbury, CT: Franklin Watts, 2001.

Vogt, Gregory L. *Deep Space Astronomy*. Brookfield, CT: Twenty-First Century Books, 1999.

———. *Disasters in Space Exploration*. Brookfield, CT: The Millbrook Press, 2001.

Magazines

Astronomy
http://www.astronomy.com

Sky & Telescope
http://www.skypub.com

Online

Alpha Centauri's Universe
http://www.to-scorpio.com/index.htm
A good site for basic information about the solar system.

Magellan
http://www.jpl.nasa.gov/magellan/
The official NASA *Magellan* spacecraft site.

NASA Spacelink
http://spacelink.msfc.nasa.gov/index.html
Gateway to many NASA Web sites about the Sun and planets.

Nine Planets
http://www.nineplanets.org
Detailed information about the Sun, the planets, and all the moons, including many photos and useful links to other Web sites.

Planet Orbits
http://www.alcyone.de
A free software program that allows the user to see the positions of all the planets in the solar system at one time.

Planet Visibility
http://www.alcyone.de
A free software program that allows users to find out when they can see a particular planet and where to look for it in the sky.

Solar System Simulator
http://space.jpl.nasa.gov/
An amazing Web site that allows the visitor to travel to all the planets and moons and to create their own views of these distant worlds.

Organizations

American Astronomical Society
2000 Florida Avenue NW
Suite 400
Washington, DC 20009-1231
http://www.AAS.org

Association of Lunar and Planetary Observers
P.O. Box 171302
Memphis, TN 38187-1302
http://www.lpl.arizona.edu/alpo/

Astronomical Society of the Pacific
390 Ashton Avenue
San Francisco, CA 94112
http://www.aspsky.org

The Planetary Society
65 N. Catalina Avenue
Pasadena, CA 91106
http://planetary.org